Usborne
# Build your own
# ALIENS
## Sticker Book

Designed by Marc Maynard
Written by Simon Tudhope
Illustrated by Gong Studios

## Contents

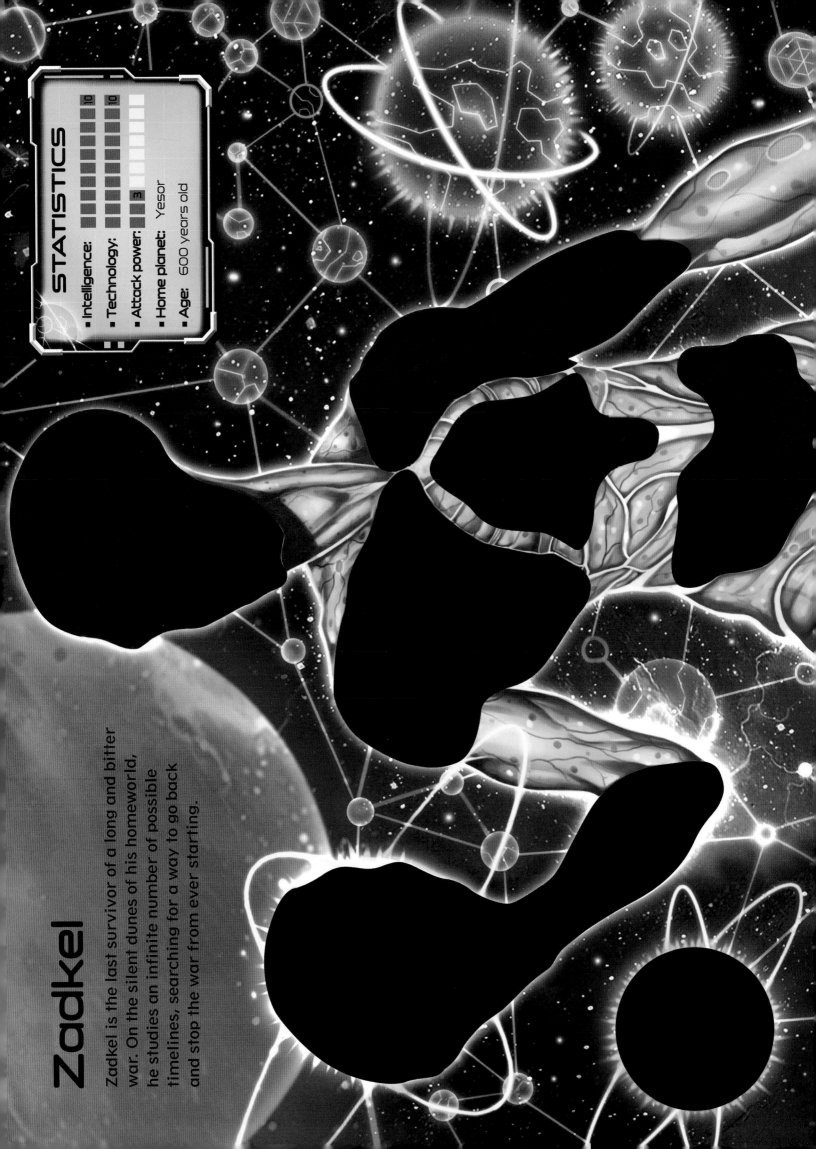

# Zadkel

Zadkel is the last survivor of a long and bitter war. On the silent dunes of his homeworld, he studies an infinite number of possible timelines, searching for a way to go back and stop the war from ever starting.

# Kreegils

Meet the tiniest crewmates on *SS Titan* – a cruise ship that sails around the Corona Nebula. Passengers hear their strange chatter late at night, as the kreegils scuttle through the service pipes, making repairs.

## STATISTICS

- Intelligence: 7
- Technology: 5
- Attack power: 2
- Home planet: Kreeg
- Age: 5 months old

# Typhon

Typhon picks through the wreckage of his latest prize. From his hidden base, he shoots down spaceships and scavenges parts to sell on the black market. His robo-eye flashes as it locates a graviton core. He grunts in satisfaction – that'll fetch a pretty sum.

STATISTICS

- Intelligence: 7
- Technology: 7
- Attack power: 7
- Home planet: Saurus
- Age: 110 years old

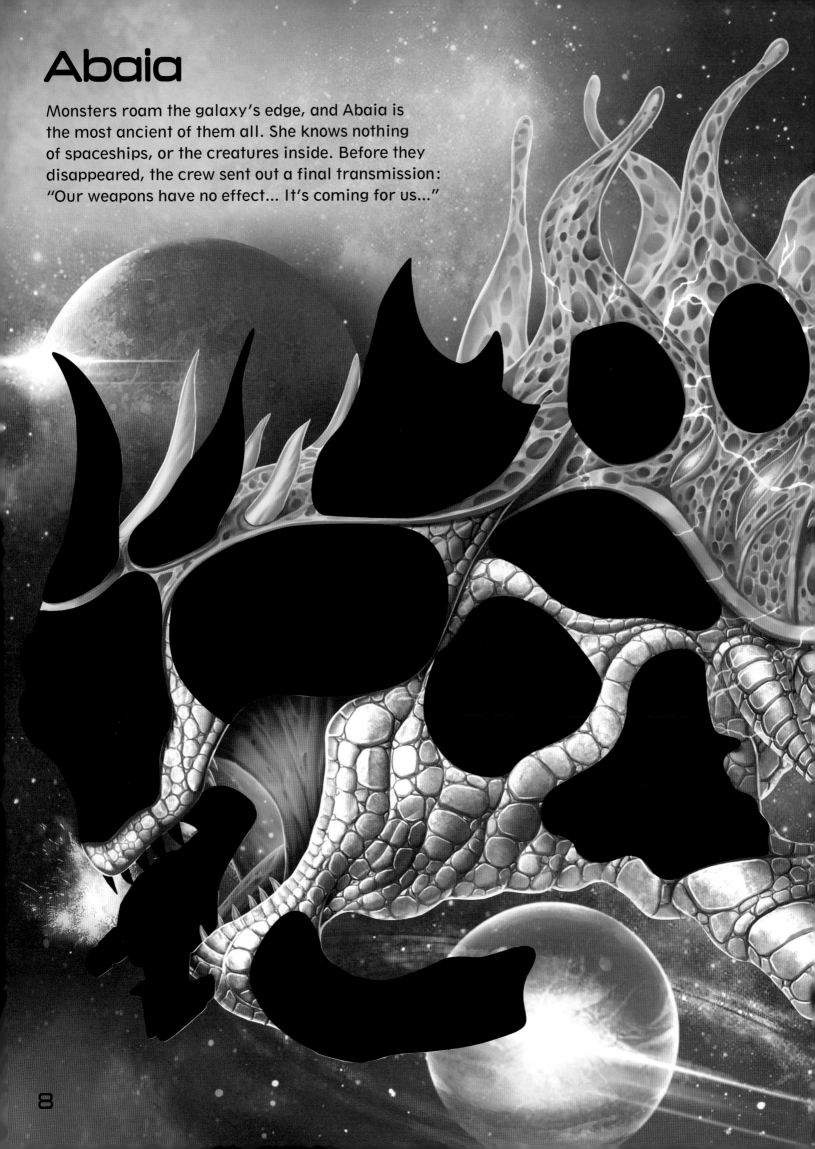

# Abaia

Monsters roam the galaxy's edge, and Abaia is
the most ancient of them all. She knows nothing
of spaceships, or the creatures inside. Before they
disappeared, the crew sent out a final transmission:
"Our weapons have no effect... It's coming for us..."

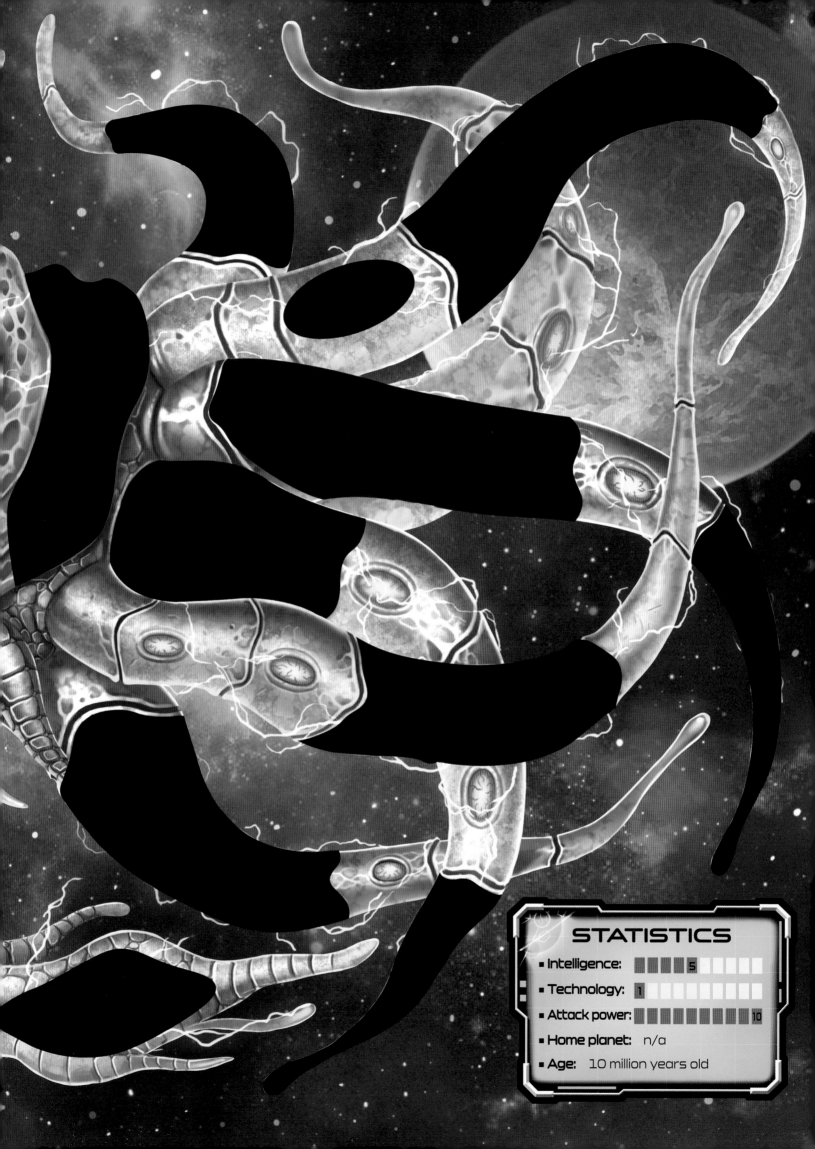

STATISTICS

- Intelligence: 5
- Technology: 1
- Attack power: 10
- Home planet:  n/a
- Age:  10 million years old

# Yegoda

A traitor in the royal court of the Byzan Empire is sending vital information to the rebels. But the spymaster general has found out their identity at last. Her eyes narrow as her winged agent whispers their name. "You're mine, now," she hisses.

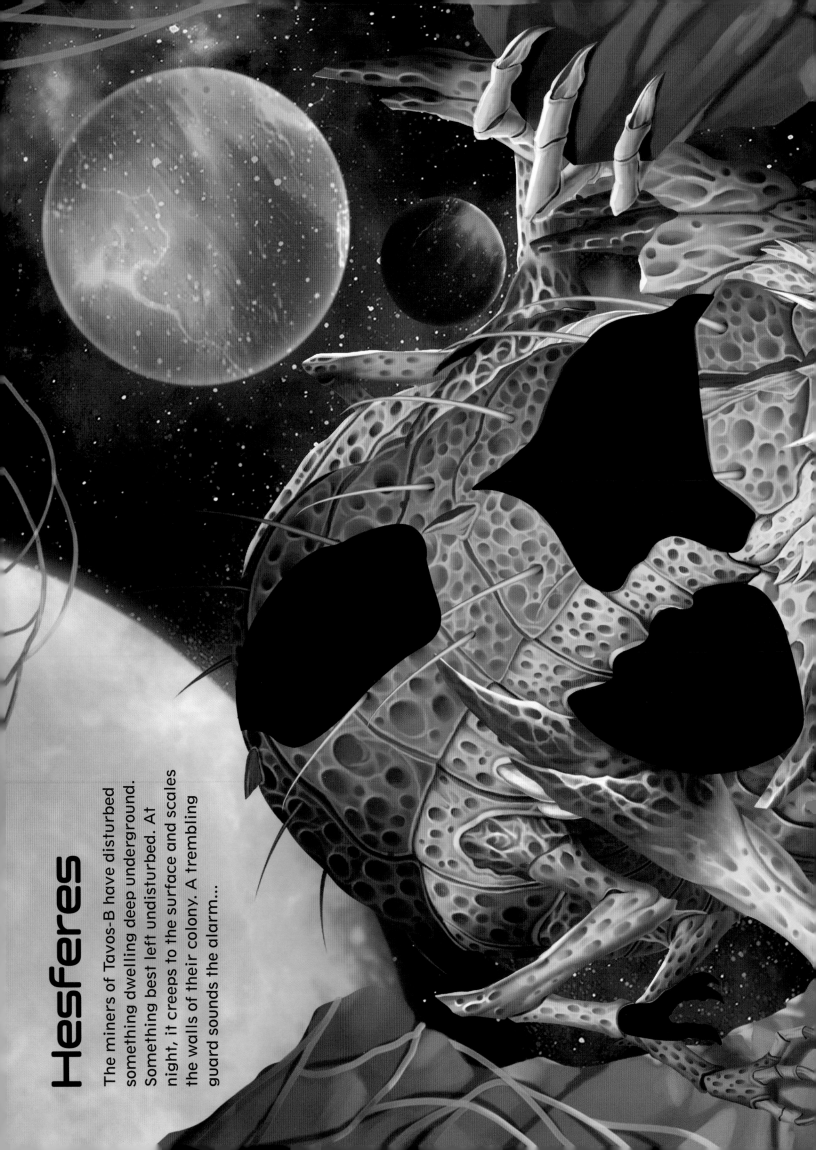

# Hesferes

The miners of Tavos-B have disturbed something dwelling deep underground. Something best left undisturbed. At night, it creeps to the surface and scales the walls of their colony. A trembling guard sounds the alarm...

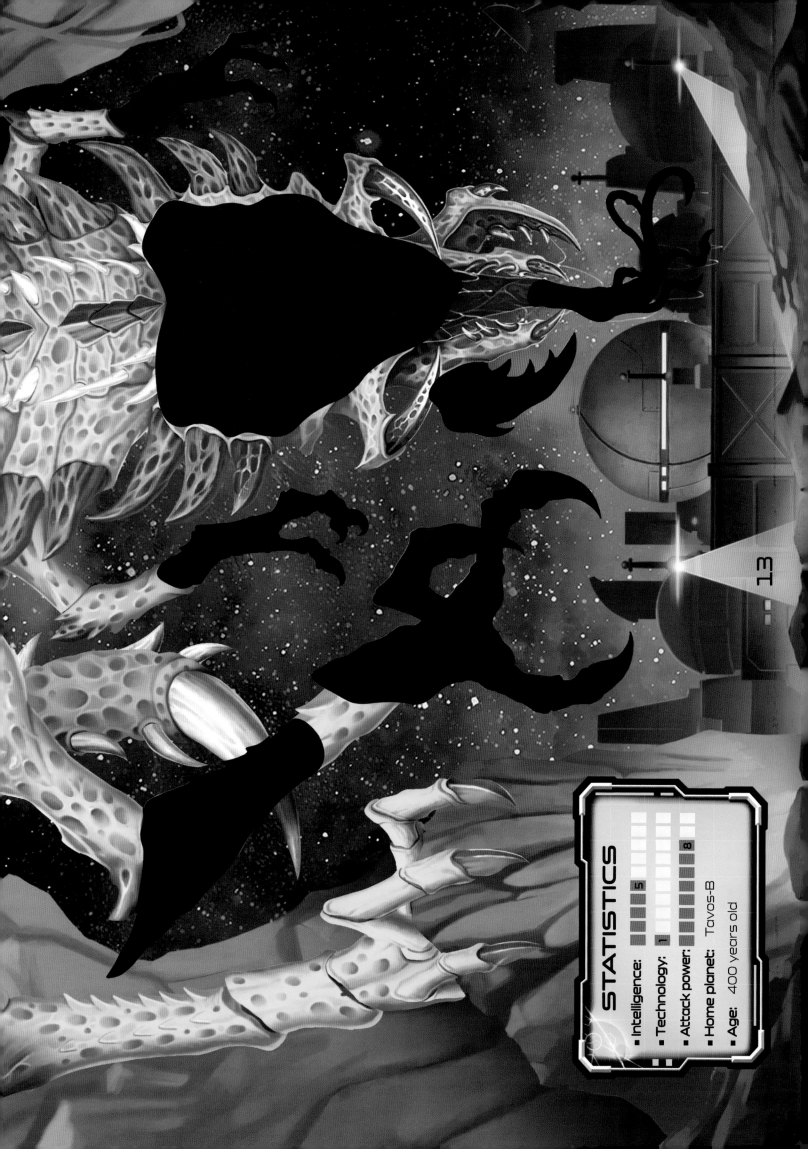

## STATISTICS

- Intelligence: 5
- Technology: 1
- Attack power: 8
- Home planet: Tavos-B
- Age: 400 years old

# Vodan

Vodan and her rebels have been driven back to their mountain base. But suddenly the enemy assault wavers. Dark shapes are swooping down from the sky... the space pirates have answered her call for help! "It's not over yet," she snarls.

**STATISTICS**

- Intelligence: 8
- Technology: 7
- Attack power: 7
- Home planet: Parvine
- Age: 80 years old

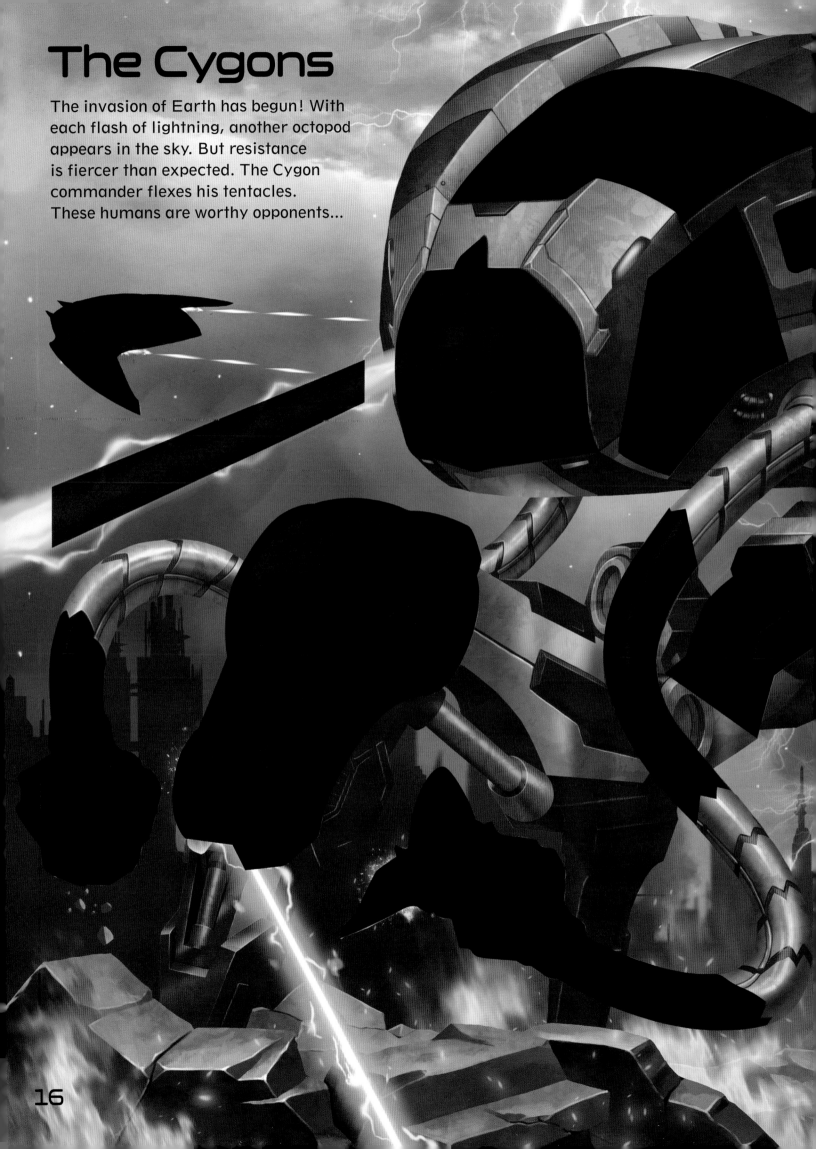

# The Cygons

The invasion of Earth has begun! With each flash of lightning, another octopod appears in the sky. But resistance is fiercer than expected. The Cygon commander flexes his tentacles. These humans are worthy opponents...

## STATISTICS

- **Intelligence:** 8
- **Technology:** 8
- **Attack power:** 8
- **Home planet:** Cygos
- **Age:** 90 years old

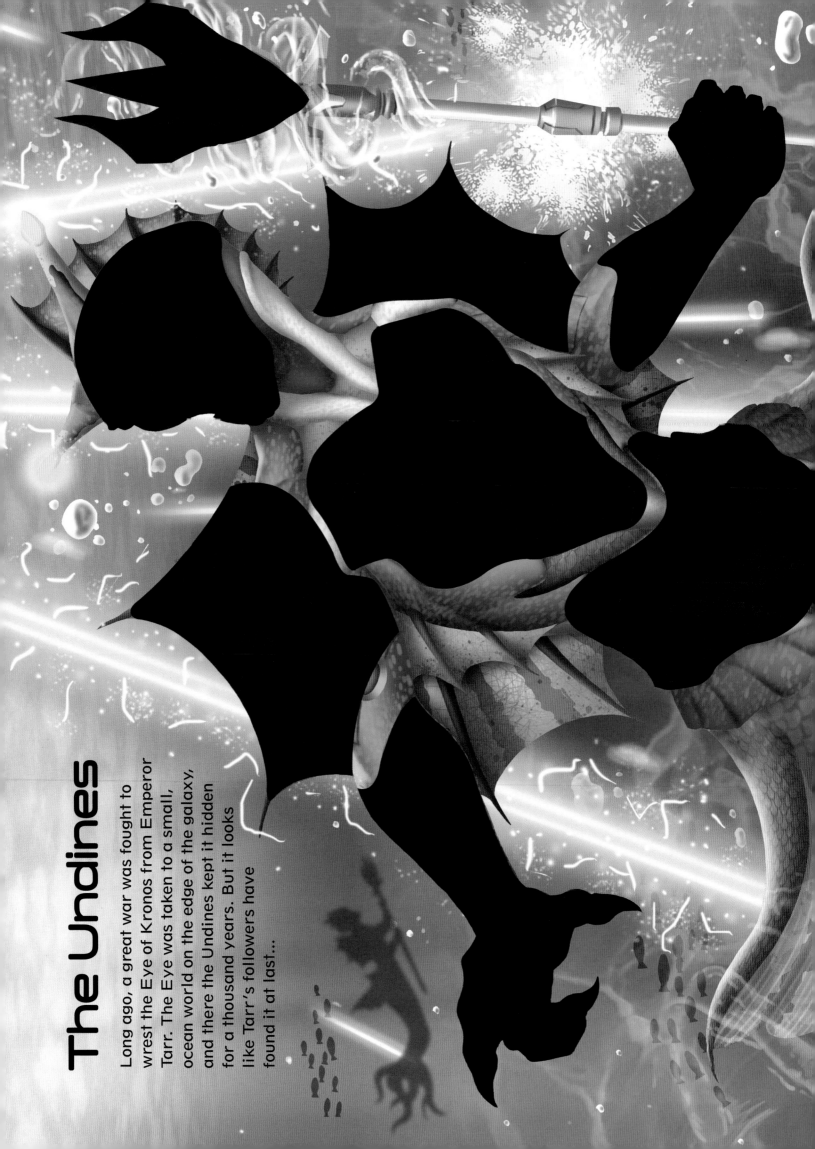

# The Undines

Long ago, a great war was fought to wrest the Eye of Kronos from Emperor Tarr. The Eye was taken to a small, ocean world on the edge of the galaxy, and there the Undines kept it hidden for a thousand years. But it looks like Tarr's followers have found it at last...

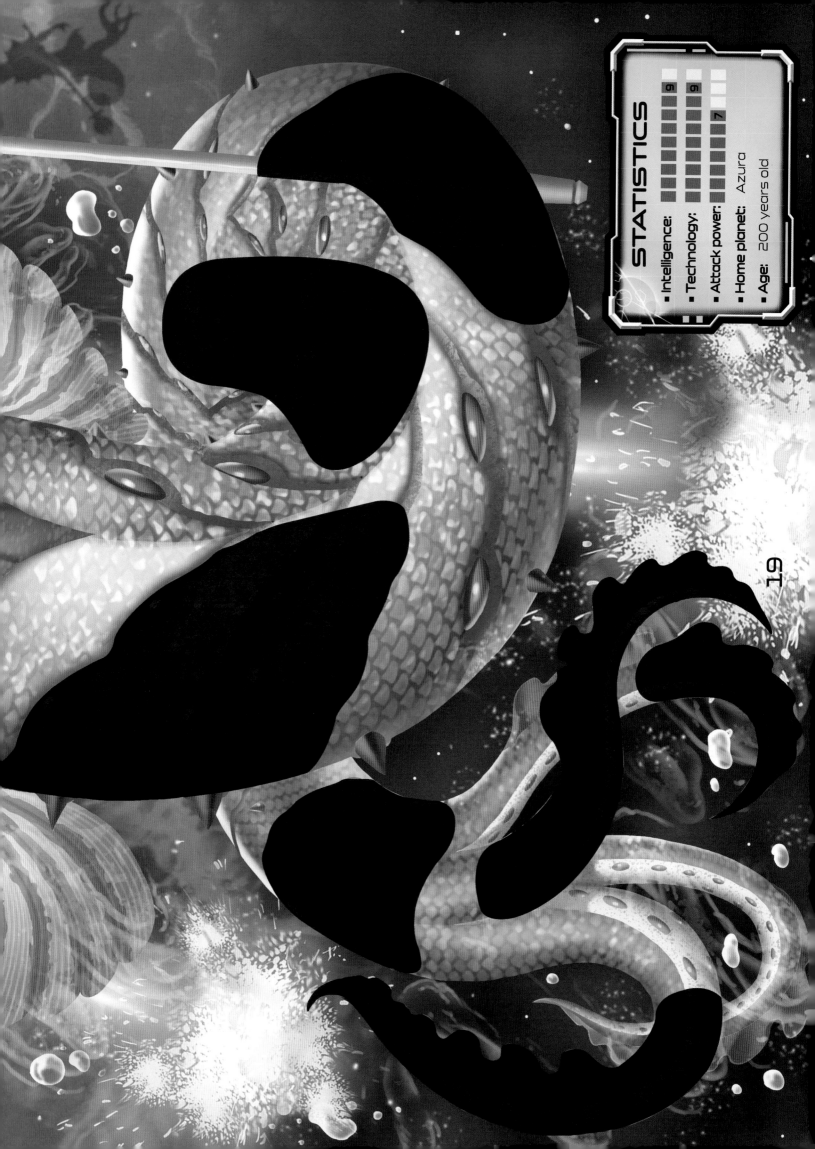

**STATISTICS**

- Intelligence: 9
- Technology: 9
- Attack power: 7
- Home planet: Azura
- Age: 200 years old

# Barazzin

The galaxy's most famous outlaw has been caught in an ambush. But he's not going down without a fight! Rolling through the smallest of gaps he breaks free and fires the thrusters. Entering hyperspace in 5... 4... 3...

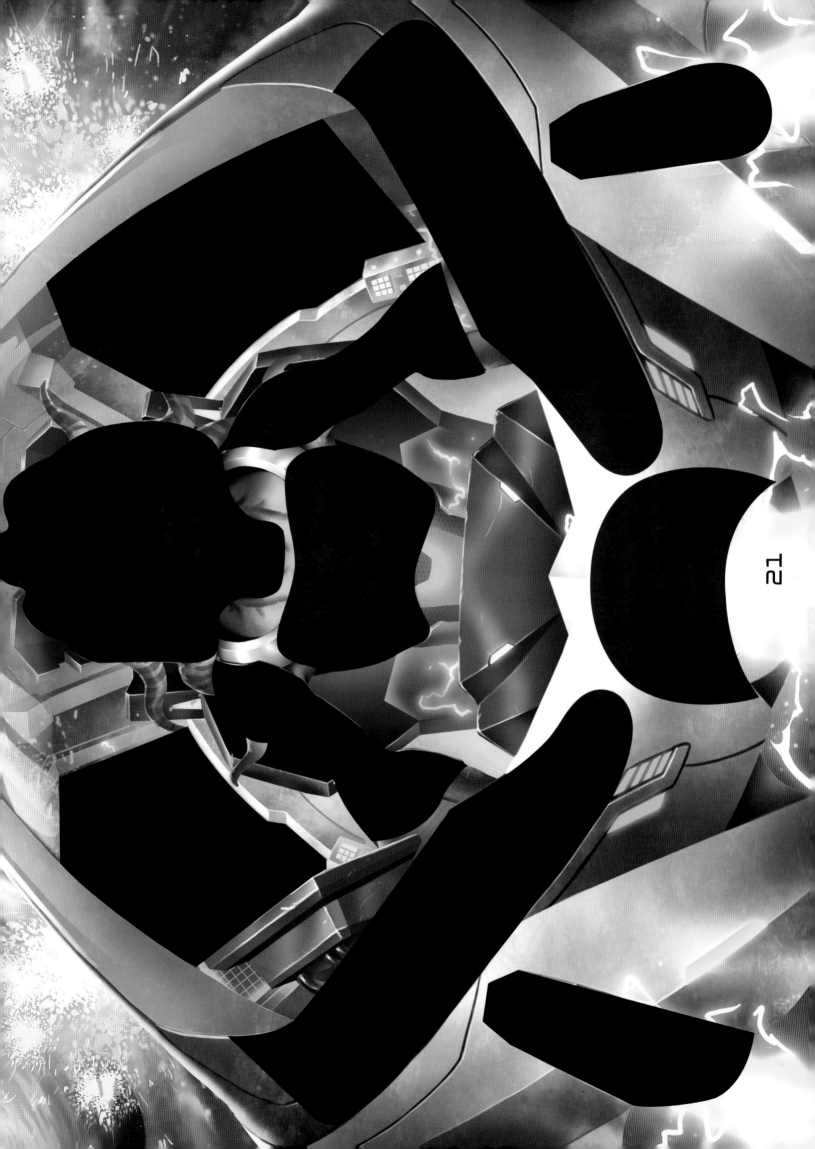

21

# Gritcher

Gritcher freezes. Beneath the insects' drone she hears the faintest hiss behind her back. She spins and leaps with all claws raised. Only the strongest and quickest survive for long in the swamps of Gucifer-6!

STATISTICS

- Intelligence: 6
- Technology: 3
- Attack power: 7
- Home planet: Gucifer-6
- Age: 30 years old

23

# Glossary

- **colony:** a settlement on another planet

- **drone:** a buzzing sound

- **dune:** a hill of sand, formed by the wind

- **hyperspace:** a place where you can travel faster than the speed of light

- **infinite:** without limit

- **nebula:** a giant space-cloud, often formed by the explosions of dying stars. It's also where new stars are born.

- **ocean world:** a planet covered entirely by water

- **scavenge:** pick up abandoned objects

- **timeline:** a diagram of historical events

- **transmission:** a message

Edited by Sam Taplin

Digital manipulation by Keith Furnival

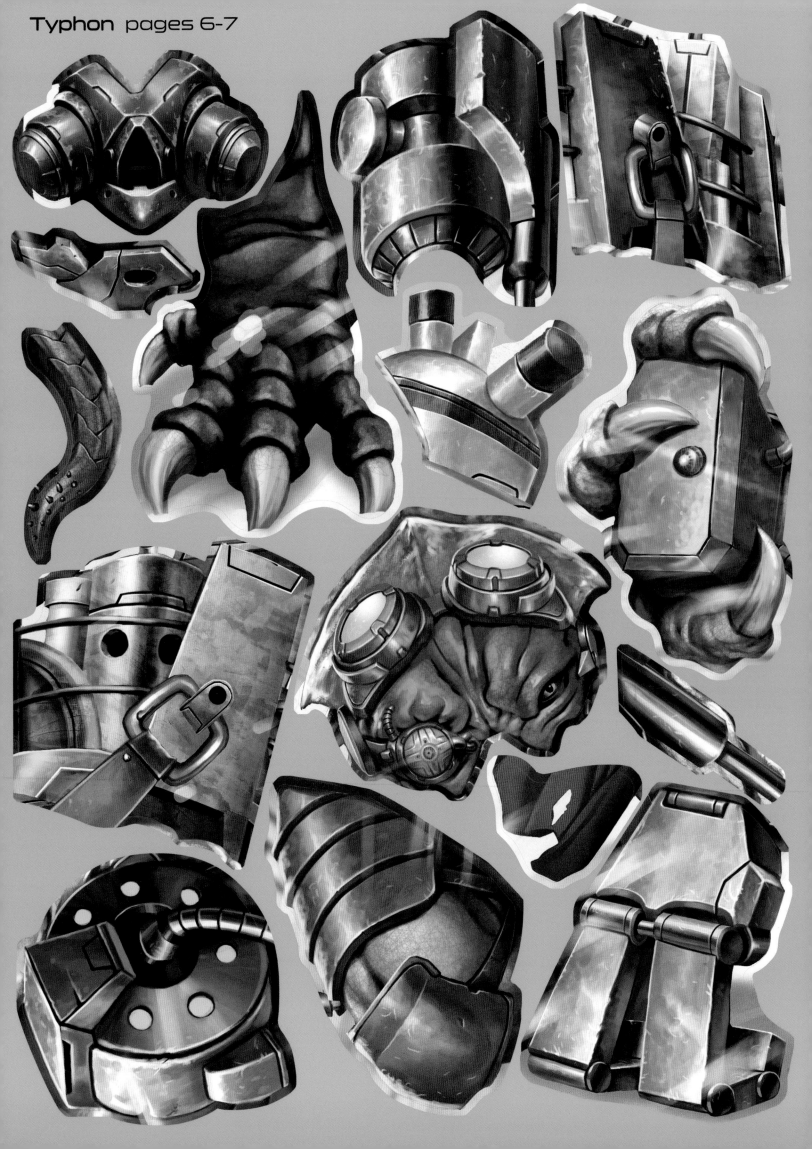

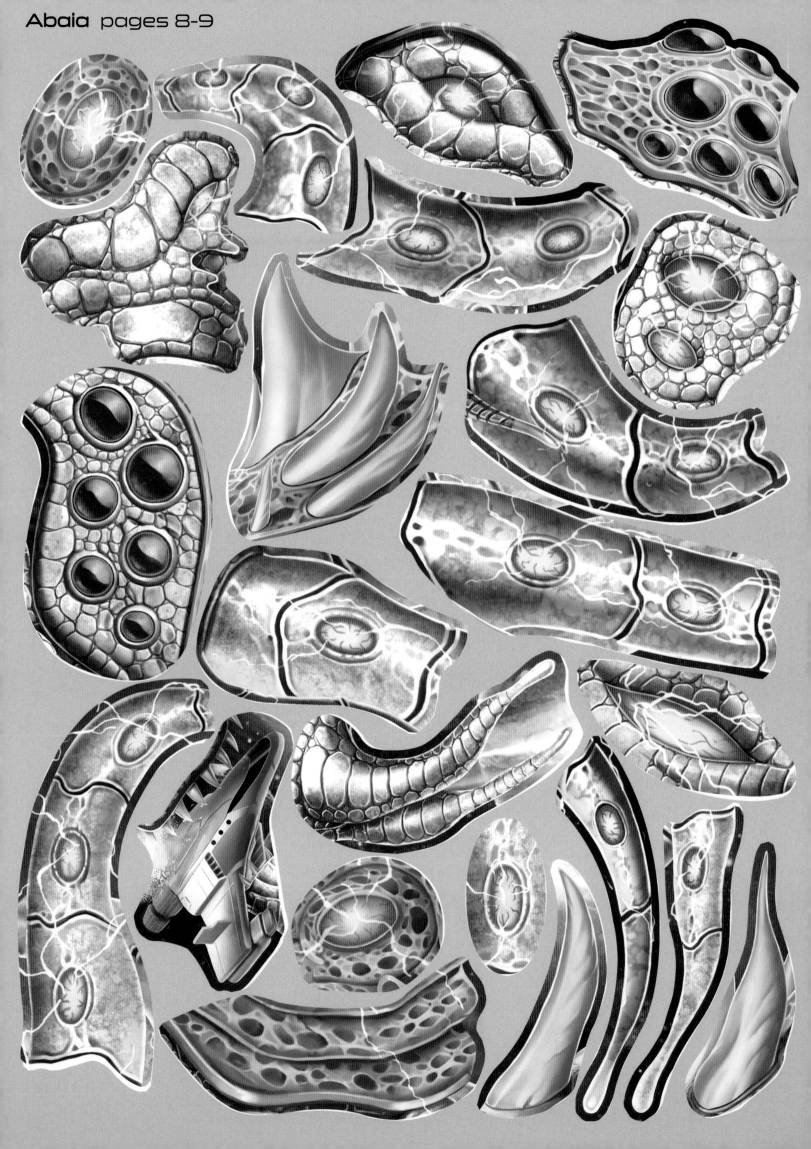

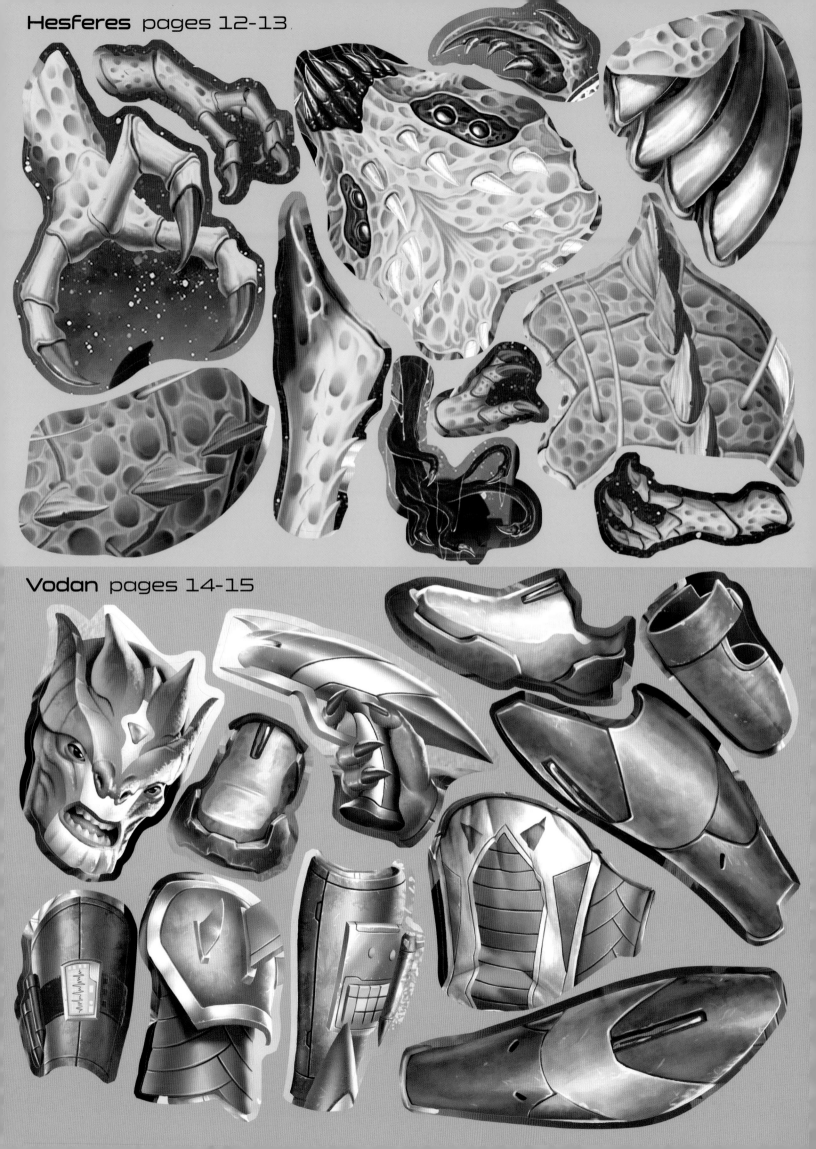

Vodan pages 14-15